LifeCycles

Joey to Kangaroo

Camilla de la Bédoyère

QED Publishing

Words in **bold** are explained in the glossary on page 22.

Copyright © QED Publishing 2009

First published in the UK in 2009 by
QED Publishing
A Quarto Group company
226 City Road
London EC1V 2TT

www.qed-publishing.co.uk

A catalogue record for this book is available from the British Library.

ISBN 978 1 84835 225 4

Printed and bound in China

Author Camilla de la Bédoyère
Editor Angela Royston
Designer and Picture Researcher Melissa Alaverdy

Publisher Steve Evans
Creative Director Zeta Davies
Managing Editor Amanda Askew

Picture credits
(t=top, b=bottom, l=left, r=right, c=centre, fc=front cover)

Corbis 11 Martin Harvey Gallo Images

FLPA 12–13 Gerard Lacz, 16 Janet Finch

fotoLibra 8t Guenter Lenz, 18 Guenter Lenz

Getty Images 1t Gary Randall, 5b Jeff Rotman, 6 Frank Lukasseck, 7t John W Banagan, 17b Art Wolfe, 17r Gary Randall, 19 Frank Krahmer, 24 Frank Lukasseck

NHPA 10 ANT Photo Library

Photolibrary Group 1b IFA Animals, 4 Juniors Bildarchiv, 5t M Harvey, 6–7 Juniors Bildarchiv, 8b Oxford Scientific (OSF), 8–9 John Cancalosi, 13 Harry Cutting, 20–21 IFA Animals, 23 Juniors Bildarchiv

Shutterstock 2r Eric Isselée, 14 Inc, 20b Joanne Harris and Daniel Bubnich, 21t Neale Cousland

Contents

What is a kangaroo?

Kangaroos are **mammals**. Mammals have fur and they give birth to babies, which they feed with milk.

Kangaroos belong to a strange group of mammals called **marsupials**. They give birth to babies long before the babies are fully formed.

⇦ A kangaroo gives birth to only one baby at a time.

⇦ Female lions have several babies at the same time.

⇩Dolphins are mammals that live in the sea.

Most mammal mothers keep their babies inside their body until they are fully formed. Most mammals have several babies at a time.

Animals with pouches

A marsupial baby is tiny when it is born. A marsupial mother has a special **pouch**. She keeps the baby in her pouch while it grows bigger.

There are nearly 300 different types of marsupial. Most of them live in Australia or South America.

⇐ Virginia opossums live in North America. They have up to 13 babies at a time.

Red kangaroos are the largest marsupials in the world. Kangaroos have long, strong legs that are perfect for jumping across Australia's wide **grasslands**.

⇩A young kangaroo is carried safely in its mother's pouch.

⇧Koalas are marsupials that climb trees.

The story of a kangaroo

A baby kangaroo is called a **joey**. When it is born, a joey is not much bigger than a fingernail.

The **newborn** joey makes an incredible journey to reach its mother's pouch.

The story of how a living thing changes and grows is called a **life cycle**.

⇨A kangaroo's life cycle has three stages.

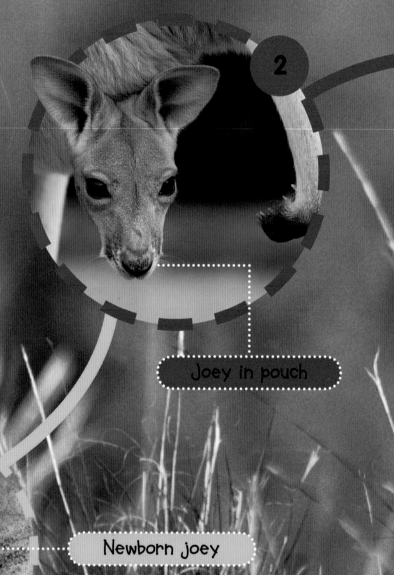

2

Joey in pouch

1

Newborn joey

3

Adult kangaroo

Fighting jacks

Before a female kangaroo can give birth, she has to **mate** with a male kangaroo. Male kangaroos are known as bucks, boomers, old men and jacks.

⇩Red kangaroo males have reddish fur, but females have grey fur.

When jacks want to mate with females, they fight with one another. They use their front paws to hit, or box, each other.

The winning jack scares the other males away. Then he mates with the females.

⇨Fighting jacks kick each other with their enormous back legs.

A new life begins

When a male kangaroo and female kangaroo mate, the male **fertilizes** a tiny egg inside the female's body.

⇩The male and female kangaroos get ready to mate.

Only a fertilized egg can grow into a new joey.

The joey grows inside the female's body for nearly five weeks.

When the female is ready to give birth, she cleans her pouch.

⇧ Before a female gives birth, she licks a path across her belly to her pouch.

13

Joey on the move

Newborn joeys have strong arms, but their legs and tails have not yet grown.

As soon as the joey is born, it begins a difficult climb. It grips its mother's fur and pulls itself up her body to her pouch. The mother does not help her joey.

⇨ The arrows show the joey's journey. This is the path the mother licked across her belly.

Inside the pouch, the joey finds its mother's **nipple**. It begins to feed on the milk her body makes.

2

⇨ This joey is four weeks old. It is blind and still has no fur, but it is growing and changing all the time.

Ready, steady, grow!

Inside the pouch, a joey feeds, sleeps and grows. It is a cosy place for a young animal.

The joey stays attached to its mother's nipple for about ten weeks. The joey changes slowly at first. It is nearly five months old before it can open its eyes.

Then the joey pushes its head out and looks around. It will soon be ready to leave the pouch.

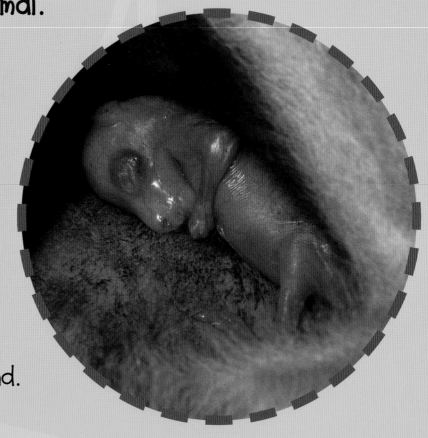

⇧ For the first few months, the joey slowly grows bigger.

⇨A joey watches what goes on around it.

⇨The mother cleans her joey and the pouch by licking them with her long tongue.

17

Leaving the pouch

When it is about six months old, the joey leaves the pouch for the first time.

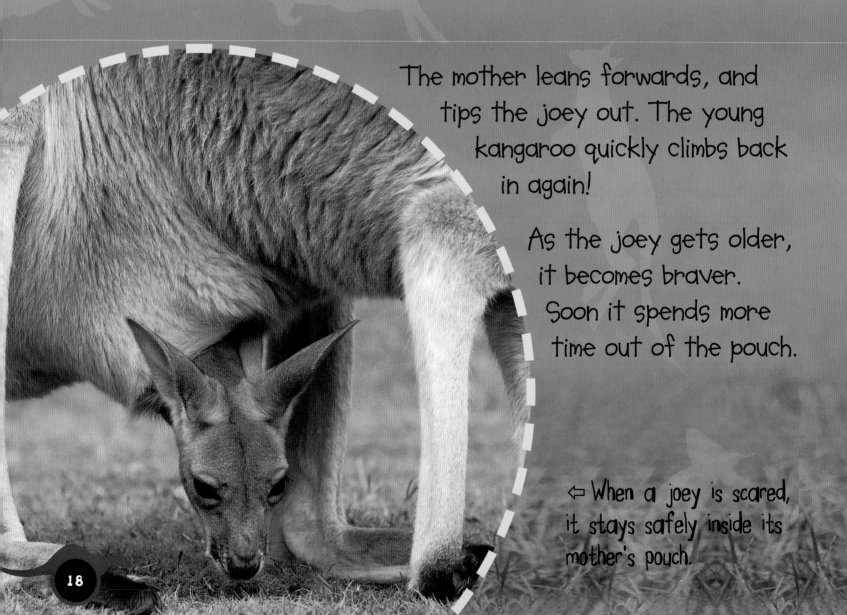

The mother leans forwards, and tips the joey out. The young kangaroo quickly climbs back in again!

As the joey gets older, it becomes braver. Soon it spends more time out of the pouch.

⇐ When a joey is scared, it stays safely inside its mother's pouch.

Joeys return to the pouch for milk or to sleep. When the joey is about eight months old, the mother stops it climbing into her pouch. A new joey is growing there now.

⇩Although this joey is too big to get into the pouch, it still feeds on its mother's milk.

How kangaroos live

Young kangaroos feed on milk until they are about one year old, but they eat solid food, too.

Kangaroos **graze** on plants, such as grass. They can travel long distances in search of food and water.

⇦ Kangaroos spend much of their time eating.

When they are 18 to 24 months old, kangaroos are ready to mate. Then the story of a new life cycle begins.

⇧ Between two and ten kangaroos live together in a group, called a **mob**.

⇦ When an adult kangaroo is scared, it quickly bounds to safety.

Glossary

Fertilize
When a special male cell changes a female's egg so that it can grow into a new living thing.

Grasslands
Areas of land covered mainly by grass and bushes.

Graze
When animals eat grass.

Joey
A baby kangaroo.

Life cycle
The story of how a living thing changes from birth to death and how it produces young.

Mammal
An animal that has fur and feeds its young with milk.

Marsupial
A type of mammal that gives birth to very small young. Some marsupials keep their young safe in a pouch.

Mate
When a male animal fertilizes a female animal's egg or eggs.

Mob
A group of kangaroos.

Newborn
A baby just after it is born.

Nipple
The place on a female mammal's body where milk comes out.

Pouch
Part of a female kangaroo's body. A pouch is shaped like a big pocket, and is a safe place for a joey to grow.

Index

Notes for parents and teachers

Look through the book and talk about the pictures. Read the captions and ask questions about other things in the photographs that have not been included in the captions.

Use an atlas to find the places mentioned in this book. Search the Internet for images of other marsupials and see how many different kinds you can find.

Joeys need care and protection, just like human babies. Talk about the care and protection newborn babies need, and how their families provide those things.

Be prepared for questions about human life cycles. There are plenty of books available for this age group that can help you give age-appropriate explanations.

Talking about a child's own family helps them to link life processes, such as reproduction, to their own experience. Drawing a simple family tree, looking at family photo albums and sharing family stories with grandparents are fun ways to engage children.